MIND-BOGGLING
SCIENCE

Clare Oliver

213

D1325055

Operation Alien
In the 1990s, film footage was found showing
a medical examination of an alien, supposedly
captured by the US Air Force almost 50 years before.
Did they discover something truly out of this world?

WHAT IS GRAVITY?

We can't see it, but it's everywhere. Gravity makes a skydiver fall to the ground rather than float upwards. It pulls everyone and everything on Earth towards the ground and gives things weight. Gravity comes from the Latin word *gravitas*, meaning heaviness.

Skydiver

SCIENCE QUIZ

In which book did Newton explain his ideas about gravity?

a) *Principia*
b) *Gravity's Rainbow*
c) *Notes from an Orchard*

Where do you weigh more, on Earth or on the Moon?

a) on Earth
b) on the Moon
c) you weigh the same in both places

Which type of execution does not rely on gravity?

a) hanging
b) guillotine
c) electrocution

(answers on page 32)

GALILEO & GRAVITY

Galileo Galilei was one of the first scientists to investigate the mysteries of gravity. He used to climb the Leaning Tower of Pisa in Italy and drop things on to the public square below. He proved that objects of different weights fall at the same speed. Gravity makes falling objects accelerate at a constant speed of 9 metres per second.

NUTTY NEWTON

The real brainbox on gravity was Sir Isaac Newton, a seventeenth-century English physicist and mathematician. His law of gravity states that every bit of matter in the universe attracts other matter. The force of this attraction depends on mass – heavier things having greater pulling power.

GROOVY GRAVITY

A magical power is at work right now. It keeps you from falling off your chair - most of the time! - and stops you from floating off into space. What is this invisible force? Gravity, that's what!

Astronauts in zero gravity on the space shuttle

IS THERE GRAVITY IN SPACE?

In space, astronauts become weightless because there is no gravity. They float about inside their spacecraft and so does everything else – including their dinner! On the Moon the gravity is much weaker than on Earth. That's why it's virtually impossible to walk normally on the Moon, and why the astronauts bounce along like kangaroos.

BONCE BOUNCE

Super-boffin Isaac Newton came up with his theory of gravity after an apple fell on his head.

SUPER SPEED

Scientists often need complex words to describe brilliant ideas. So it's no surprise that the simple act of gathering speed has a special name - acceleration. But, talk to a scientist and you'll soon discover speed is not as simple as it may first appear.

VELOCITY VERSUS SPEED

Scientists have two different measurements for how fast objects travel. Speed is how far an object moves in a certain time. Velocity is speed in one direction, so it changes every time the speed or direction changes. On a roller coaster, your speed is constant (you travel the length of the ride in a set amount of time), but your velocity keeps changing as you point in different directions.

Thrust SSC

JUST THRUST

Most of us enjoy speed for what it is – a thrilling ride, perhaps in a fast car or speedboat. The official one-mile (1.6-km) land-speed record is a rather zippy 1,227.985 km/h. It is held by British driver Andy Green and his superfast car, the aptly-named *Thrust SSC*. Two jet engines give the vehicle 22,680 kg of thrust – enough for the car to become the first to break the sound barrier. That easily beats the speed record on water – held by the hydroplane *Spirit of Australia*, at 556 km/h.

TO THE LIMIT

The fastest speed ever recorded on a skateboard is 89 km/h. That's twice as fast as the town speed limit for a car – phew!

SUMMING UP

Scientists work out an object's momentum with a sneaky sum. They multiply the thing's mass by its velocity. If a moving object crashes into something else, chances are it will come to a sudden halt but transfer its momentum to the object it hit. That is what happens if you play ball with a bat. The momentum of the bat passes to the ball and makes it fly through the air.

MAGIC MOMENTUM

On that roller-coaster ride, momentum is what keeps your bellyful of lunch moving in the same direction, even after the rest of your body has changed course! Yup – that funny feeling when your stomach jumps!

SCIENCE QUIZ

At what speed does sound travel through the air?

a) 157 metres per second
b) 331.3 metres per second
c) 1,000 metres per second

Which was the first passenger plane to break the sound barrier?

a) *Concorde*
b) Boeing *707*
c) *Harrier* Jump Jet

Which word means increasing speed?

a) acceleration
b) velocity
c) momentum

(answers on page 32)

A roller coaster gathers momentum

SCIENCE QUIZ

Which of these three metals is the most magnetic?

a) gold
b) iron
c) magnesium

What is the force that surrounds a magnet?

a) a magnetic cushion
b) a magnetic field
c) a magnetic park

What is a scientist who specialises in magnetism called?

a) magus
b) magician
c) magnetist

(answers on page 32)

MAGNETIC MACHINES

Magnets aren't just for fun. Some of them do seriously hard work. Electromagnets are the most powerful magnets of all and can pick up whopping great weights. They are made by passing electricity through a large coil of wire, which makes the coil behave like a magnet. The biggest electromagnets are strong enough to lift a lorry.

SIDE-SPLITTING

If you could break a magnet in half – you would be amazingly strong! You might think you'd end up with one 'north' magnet and one 'south'. In fact, each half would be a completely new magnet with its own north and south poles!

WHICH WAY IS NORTH?

If you're an explorer in a very snowy place, one way to work out which pole you're near is by looking at the animals. If you see a polar bear, you're in the Arctic (North Pole); but if you see a penguin, you're in the Antarctic (South Pole). Or, you could simply use a compass! Our planet is like a giant magnet with a north and a south. The compass needle is always magnetically attracted towards the North Pole.

At the South Pole

MAGNETIC ATTRACTION

The mysterious power of magnets has fascinated people since ancient times, but it was not until 1820 that Danish scientist Hans Christian Oersted discovered that electricity and magnetism have an effect on one another.

HOW ATTRACTIVE!

Every magnet has two poles, a north and a south. Hold the north pole of one magnet next to the south pole of another and they'll want to stick together. The force pulling them is magnetism. Hold two north poles together and you'll find they push against each other. So, the basic rule of magnetism is that opposites attract and equals repel. Iron filings clinging to a magnet become mini-magnets themselves, able to carry other iron filings that aren't even touching the magnet!

Magnet attracting iron filings

LODES O' MAGNETS

Magnets take their name from Magnesia, a place known to the ancient Greeks. Magnetic rock called lodestone occurred naturally there.

IT'S ELECTRIFYING!

Where would we be without electricity? In the dark! Our cities would be pitch black at night. There'd be no kettles and, worst of all, no telly or computer games! Electricity is one of the most marvellous forms of energy we know.

STUNNING STATIC

Have you ever heard a crackle when you're brushing your hair? That's static electricity. When two things rub together, tiny particles called electrons move from one to the other (from your hair to the brush bristles). Because your hair has lost electrons, it becomes positively charged and because the brush has gained electrons, it becomes negatively charged. Static electricity can even make your hair stand on end. A Van de Graaff generator (right) gives out a positive charge. Touch it, and all your hairs become positively charged, so each one tries to push away from the next!

BATTERY SARNIE

Electrical energy is measured in volts, after Count Alessandro Volta. He made the first-ever battery by sandwiching paper soaked in saltwater between a sheet of silver and a sheet of zinc. Yum!

CIRCUIT TRAINING

Every electrical appliance starts with a circuit – a loop of wire, or other electrical conductor, around which an electrical current can flow. Circuits with batteries work with direct current (DC). Generators produce alternating current (AC) that changes direction 100 times a second and is safer for big quantities of electricity.

Electricity powers our cities

LUCKY ESCAPE

In 1752, Benjamin Franklin proved that lightning is a natural form of electricity. He flew a kite in a thunderstorm with a metal key hanging from the kite's string. Lightning struck the kite and there was a spark from the key when the electric current passed down the wet string. Don't try this experiment, though – Franklin was lucky not to be fried to a frazzle!

LIGHTING UP

Thomas Edison invented the electric light bulb in 1879. To market it, he rigged up fairy lights in a park and laid on free trains for visitors. Unfortunately, hardly anyone had any electricity in their homes to power light bulbs – that's probably why Edison was also responsible for building New York City's first electrical power station.

A Van de Graaff generator

SCIENCE QUIZ

What turns mechanical motion into electricity?

a) a dynamo
b) dynamic
c) a crank

Which unit measures the strength of an electrical current?

a) amp
b) ohm
c) watt

What did the Greek word *elektron* mean?

a) warmth
b) amber
c) goddess

(answers on page 32)

PERFECT PRISM

A prism

Brainy Isaac Newton was the first scientist to write about the different colours contained in white light. He used a triangular piece of glass, called a prism, in his experiments. Each colour in white light travels at a fractionally different speed, so when it hits the glass of the prism, it refracts (bends) at a fractionally different angle. This means each colour comes out the other side along its own separate path, so it's easy to see them all. The colours, known as the spectrum, are the same colours you see in a rainbow.

The spectrum

ROUND THE BEND

Light travels at different speeds through different substances. For example, it travels through air faster than it travels through either water or glass. When light slows down it also changes direction, which is called refraction. Refraction is what makes an object in a glass of water, such as a straw, seem to bend where it meets the water.

LUMINOUS LIGHT

Light is another amazing phenomenon. Without sunlight there would be no life on Earth - and without artificial light we would all have to go to bed when the Sun goes down.

NIGHT SPY

Infrared rays of light are used by spies and soldiers to see at night. Nightsights may look like binoculars, but they allow the wearer to see infrared rays and get an owl's-eye view of the world!

View through a nightsight

INFRARED & ULTRAVIOLET

Even with a prism you can't see the full range of colours. Ultraviolet and infrared rays are at the ends of the colour spectrum and are not visible to the naked eye. Ultraviolet (UV) rays in sunlight are what makes pale skin go brown. The skin darkens to protect itself from the harmful rays. Still, on a very sunny day, most people's skin needs a little extra help, or the rays would burn it to a crisp. That's why we wear suntan lotion – it helps to protect us from UV rays.

COLOUR SENSE

People who can't see colours are colour-blind. What seems to them to be red may in fact be yellow, and what seems to be yellow could be green. More men are colour-blind than women.

STARGAZERS

Some of the first-ever scientists were astronomers.
These pioneers discovered patterns in the movements of the
twinkling stars - and identified other heavenly bodies, too.

CONSTELLATIONS

Some stars are visible to the naked eye.
Others can only be seen with a telescope.
Look at the night sky regularly and you'll
see – as the ancient Greeks did – that stars
are clustered in groups. Some of these
constellations are associated with signs of
the zodiac, such as Cancer (the Crab)
or Sagittarius (the Archer).

SPACE SNOWBALLS

Comets are great balls of dust and ice which
orbit the Sun at speeds up to 2,376,000 km/h.
Most never come close to the Sun, but those
that do melt a bit and develop a long trailing
tail of gas and dust.

ASTRONOMICAL!

No one knows for sure,
but there are about
100,000 million
stars in our galaxy,
the Milky Way –
that's enough for
everyone on Earth
to have 18 all
to themselves.

CALLING ALL COMETS

Comet Hale-Bopp

Many comets are named after the first people who saw them. Halley's Comet, which travels at 240,00 km/h, is named after the eighteenth-century English astronomer, Edmond Halley. It last came close enough to the Earth to be seen with the naked eye in 1986.

But the most spectacular comet of recent times was Comet Hale-Bopp, which appeared in our skies in 1997.

SPACE SPECS

Astronomers use very complicated glasses, called telescopes, to see objects far away in space. Super-scientist Galileo was the first person to use a telescope to observe the stars. Sadly, he was so fascinated by the sky, he went blind from looking at the Sun.

Radio telescope

NEW VIEW

The Very Large Telescope (VLT) in Chile is the biggest on Earth. Actually, it's seven telescopes, not just one! Each telescope is angled slightly differently and what they see is compared by computer to create a spot-on view. When the VLT is completed in 2001, it will have the power to see something as small as a man standing on the Moon!

SCIENCE QUIZ

Which ancient Greek described the constellations?

a) Ptolemy
b) Aristotle
c) Stavros the Elder

Which solo star (and group) shines most brightly in our sky?

a) Sirius (Canis)
b) Pollux (Gemini)
c) Betelgeux (Orion)

What is an exploding star called?

a) a nebula cloud
b) a supernova
c) a white dwarf

(answers on page 32)

ANYBODY THERE?

Could there really be aliens? The ancient Chinese recorded seeing strange flying objects as long ago as 1914 BC and every year, there are hundreds of reported sightings of unidentified flying objects (UFOs).

SCIENCE QUIZ

What does SETI stand for?

a) Searching Earth for Terrestrial Invaders
b) Search for Extra-Terrestrial Intelligence
c) Society of Extra-Terrestrial Invertebrates

When was the phrase 'flying saucer' coined?

a) 1847
b) 1907
c) 1947

What is a light-year?

a) a million years
b) 365 days in outer space
c) the distance light travels in a year — almost 10 million million km

(answers on page 32)

ALIEN HOAX

In 1947, a strange craft was seen to crash near a top-secret airbase in Roswell, New Mexico. The US Air Force said it was a weather balloon but some people still believe it was an alien craft. There were rumours that a body from the wreckage had been taken back to the base. In the 1990s, film footage was found that showed the 'alien' being cut open and examined, but the film proved to be a fake – one sharp-eyed viewer spotted a modern phone in the background.

The Roswell alien

INTERSTELLAR TRAVEL

There have been some wicked films about travelling to distant galaxies, but today's spacecraft travel so slowly that the crew would be long dead before they reached their destination. In the *Star Trek* films, *The Starship Enterprise* runs on an anti-matter drive. Scientists know that if anti-matter met matter it would cause an explosion 1,000 times greater than any nuclear explosion. They just need to work out how to produce and control this energy – and we'd be able to travel to distant stars, and maybe meet alien life forms!

A SHOUT GOING OUT...

How could we communicate with aliens if they *did* exist? On Earth alone, there are more languages than countries! Inside the space probe *Voyager 1*, heading out into deep space, is a gold-plated record called 'Sounds of the Earth'. It plays greetings in 60 languages and has natural sounds of the Earth to give a clue about what life is like here.

...A MESSAGE COMING IN?

The Arecibo dish in Puerto Rico picks up radio signals from far into the Galaxy. Its job is to map faraway planets and stars, but maybe one day it will pick up an alien broadcast! Problem is, the signal will have taken light years to reach us, so any message is likely to have come from a civilisation that died out millions of years ago!

COSMIC!

Some scientists believe time travel may be possible. They think cosmic tunnels called wormholes link different regions of space-time.

BIG BLUNDERS

If you suspect those clever clogs of science never get anything wrong, think again – they do. But even scientific mistakes sometimes lead to devilishly good discoveries.

MARS MISTAKE

When *Climate Orbiter* was launched on the back of *Delta II 7425* in December 1998, NASA scientists had high hopes. The space probe's mission to Mars was intended to find out all sorts of information about the Red Planet's atmosphere and climate. But a crucial error was made. Imperial measurements are used in the USA – distances are measured in feet and miles; weights in pounds and ounces. But the computer software that helped the probe to navigate in space was working in metric measurements. As a result, the probe was 'lost' in autumn 1999. Oops!

ON THE EDGE

People haven't always thought the Earth was round. Only 600 years ago, scientists believed the Earth was flat and, that if you sailed too far, you'd fall off the edge!

ANOTHER ICE AGE?

These days, scientists are scaring us with the threat of global warming. They say that pollution is heating up the Earth, which could cause icecaps to melt, seas to rise and islands to drown. Yet, in the 1960s and '70s scientists were forecasting another ice age. After record snowfalls, scientists calculated that we must be due for another big freeze since it was 10,500 years since the last one!

Climate Orbiter launch

ANCIENT GREEK GOOF

The astronomer Ptolemy was pretty hot on most things. We still follow his lead on the constellations, but his writings about the universe contain one big misunderstanding. Around AD 127 he developed a theory that the Earth was at the centre of the solar system. We might like to think it is, but we know it's not really!

SCIENCE QUIZ

Why did Scottish-born inventor Alexander Bell black out his windows?

a) he didn't want his favourite sofa to fade
b) he wanted to invent the phone in secret
c) to block harmful rays from the Moon

Who thought magnetic fluid flows around all living things?

a) Friedrich Mesmer
b) Albert Einstein
c) Herbert Irons

What is at the centre of our solar system?

a) a black hole
b) nobody knows
c) the Sun

(answers on page 32)

HIGHLY ILLOGICAL: PHLOGISTON

Scientists spent centuries trying to find a mystery substance called 'phlogiston', which they believed was something that escaped during the burning process. They wanted to understand why a log was heavy and yet the ashes left in a fire were light, for example. What they didn't understand was that fire causes a chemical reaction and so solid matter can turn to a gas or liquid.

Making phlogiston?

17

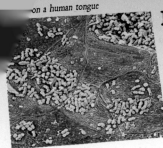
on a human tongue

PESKY PARASITES?

Did you know you are a walking hotel? Tiny little creatures are, at this very moment, going about their business on your eyelashes, tongue, teeth, belly button and just about everywhere on your body. In fact, they spend their whole life there! Bacteria multiply by feasting on your body's building blocks – cells. But not all bacteria are bad. Some do a useful job. They eat up your body wastes, such as old flakes of skin.

MOULD MAGIC

In 1928, the scientist Alexander Fleming was growing bacteria in his lab but accidentally used a slightly dirty petri dish. A mould started to grow and – hey presto! – it killed the bacteria. Penicillin is now used by doctors all over the world to kill bacterial infections.

INVASION!

Viruses get into your body through the air. If someone with a cold sneezes, you might breathe in the cold virus in tiny droplets of watery mucus in the air. Bacteria and protozoa have different methods of invasion. You might eat them by mistake in food that hasn't been cooked properly or drink them in dirty water. Once they're in your body, they attack and destroy your cells. But luckily, your immune system fights back.

GERM WARFARE

Lots of things are not visible to the naked eye but, thanks to the power of microscopes, we can now see for ourselves the wicked world of germs - including bacteria, viruses and tiny life forms called protozoa.

POWER PANTS

Russian scientists are developing space-age undies. The pants will be worn once, then in-built bacteria will break them down. That should end the squabbles over who will do the laundry on space stations!

ROTTEN LUCK

Mould is a type of fungus, as are mushrooms, toadstools and yeasts. The mushrooms we eat are only the fruiting bodies of the fungus. The rest – and the biggest part – hides under the soil and is made up of thousands of thread-like cells.

A single wheelbarrow of soil contains more fungi than there are people on Earth! Like bacteria, fungi feed on decay. That's why if you leave a tomato uneaten for too long, mould moves in to rot it.

mould takes hold

EVOLUTION REVOLUTION

One of the most important scientific questions is
'Where did we come from?' Charles Darwin,
a brilliant nineteenth-century scientist,
came up with the answer - evolution.

WE LOVE LUCY

One of the coolest archaeological finds for scientists studying human evolution was an australopithecine they called Lucy. Part of her skeleton was dug up in Ethiopia in 1974. Australopithecines may have been the lost link between apes and man. They were the first apes to come down from the trees and walk upright on two legs.

EGGS-STINCT!

When an animal can't adapt to new circumstances, it dies out. This is what doomed the dodos when people arrived on their island home of Mauritius. The people shot at the birds, while their dogs wolfed down their eggs.

ALL CHANGE, PLEASE!

The basic idea behind evolution is that animals adapt to their circumstances. It doesn't mean that a giraffe-like creature suddenly grows a long neck to reach the delicious buds at the top of trees. It means those creatures with slightly longer necks have an advantage and are more likely to survive and breed. Long-neckedness eventually becomes standard for them. Darwin called this the survival of the fittest.

APE JAPES

Human evolution

Darwin's most controversial idea was that people are descended from apes. Religious leaders of the day were furious. The theory contradicted their belief in God's Creation. It also clashed with their view that humans were special – after all, if we are related to chimps we must be little more than animals!

CODE OF LIFE

Today, scientists can prove how closely-related different animals are by examining their genes. They now know that 97 per cent of a chimp's genes are identical to a human's. Genes are made of DNA, which looks like two long strands coiled around each other. Every living cell in your body contains this secret code of special instructions to make you what you are. Only identical twins have the same DNA.

Model of DNA

BODY TALK

Universal space and time questions are for physicists and astronomers. Human biologists prefer bodies of the human kind. Your body is so awesome, it's as if there's a whole micro-universe under your skin.

CONTROL TOWER

Every single action you take is triggered by electrical messages from your brain to other parts of your body. Doctors and other scientists use all sorts of exciting technology to investigate this delicate and complex organ. Magnetic resonance imaging (MRI) is a special technique for scanning the brain. It produces fantastic photographs.

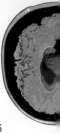

DISGUSTING DIGESTION

Just like any machine, your body needs fuel to work. Food is its fuel. The moment you pop some grub into your mouth, it sets off on an amazing journey. First, it is chewed and mixed with spit, which starts to break down the food. Then it travels to the stomach and on through your two intestines. During this process of digestion, special chemicals called enzymes work on the food to extract the goodness which is carried off via the bloodstream. Any leftover wastes are pushed out through your rectum.

SCIENCE QUIZ

How many breaths do we take in a lifetime approximately?

a) 500 million
b) 500 billion
c) 500 squillion

How fast do nerve signals move around your body?

a) 288 km/h
b) 2,888 km/h
c) 28,800 km/h

How much spit do you produce in a day?

a) 10 millilitres
b) 1.5 litres
c) 1 hectolitre

(answers on page 32)

An MRI scan of the brain

In the eighteenth century an Italian scientist, Lazzaro Spallanzani, ate his own sick to discover how enzymes digest food. He noted how it had changed t...
se...

A human skeleton

BLOOD & BONES

Your body is built around a framework of bones – your skeleton. Without bones to support everything, you'd be as flubbery as a jellyfish! Connecting the bones are muscles, powerful elastic strips that enable you to move. Blood flows through the body along tube-like arteries and veins. It is pumped around by your heart, an organ that beats more than 100,000 times a day. Other organs include your kidneys, liver, lungs and brain.

SKIN DEEP

As far as we know, the first scientist to dissect (cut open) a human body to find out what was inside, was Alcmaeon of Croton in around 500 BC.

23

AZING MEDICINE

...owledge of how the human body works has created a very special area of science – medicine. Every day, medical superheroes save millions of lives.

Scientist holding a plastic ear (right) and a fibreglass frame

SPARE PARTS

Early doctors had to lop off infected limbs before disease spread through the body. These days, superdrugs can usually save body parts but if they do get 'lost' – in war, or in an accident – a prosthesis (fake part) is fitted. You can get artificial arms, legs, noses and even ears! Most are made of special plastics, but scientists are learning to 'grow' more realistic spare parts. They can grow real human skin over a fibreglass frame, and have already succeeded in 'growing' an ear!

JENNER'S GERMS

One of the greatest medical discoveries was how to vaccinate against disease. In 1796, Edward Jenner created the first-ever vaccine by injecting children with cowpox virus. Sounds mad! But Jenner correctly guessed that in fighting off an infection a body's germ-fighting cells would then give permanent protection from it.

FIGHTING FIT

The best way to fight disease is to keep healthy. There are all sorts of ways to stay fighting fit. Exercise, sleep and being happy are all important, and so is diet. Vitamins come from fruit and vegetables and are essential for fighting disease. Energy-giving carbohydrates are found in bread, pasta and rice. Meat, fish and cheese contain protein that rebuilds damaged cells and helps you to grow. And every cell in your body needs water, so drink plenty of it.

FRUITY!

Even pirates knew vitamin C helped their bodies fight illness. English pirates were nicknamed 'limeys' because they ate limes every day.

Acupuncture needles

PINS & NEEDLES

The Chinese were pioneers of a pain-killing technique by which they stuck needles into the patient's body. Known as acupuncture, it has been practised since 2000 BC. People have even undergone heart surgery with only acupuncture to prevent pain. It is also used to treat problems to do with the mind or behaviour, such as an addiction to cigarettes.

ATOMS & ELEMENTS

Albert Einstein

If you think chemistry is the snoriest of the sciences, think again! Chemists have all sorts of fantastic jobs – from mixing up potent potions and cure-all drugs, to finding new elements.

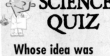

SCIENCE QUIZ

Whose idea was it to use letters to stand for chemicals?

a) Jöns Jakob Berzelius
b) Antoine Abbreviator
c) Buckminster Fuller

Who first made models of atoms using little balls?

a) Atom Boy
b) Isaac Newton
c) Friedrich Kekulé

What do chemists call laughing gas?

a) sodium chloride
b) nitrous oxide
c) lactic acid

(answers on page 32)

ELEMENTARY, MY DEAR

An element is a material that cannot be broken down into anything else. Water, for instance, can be broken down into hydrogen and oxygen so it's not an element. Hydrogen and oxygen can't be broken down into anything else, so they *are* elements.

There are more than 90 elements on Earth. For example, the element iron is found in the ground and in your blood (it makes blood red).

Chemists have created some brand-new elements in the lab, bringing the total number to over 100.

A model of a complex atomic structure

AWESOME ATOMS

Elements are made up of different tiny arrangements of atoms. Each element has a different arrangement. New Zealander Ernest Rutherford did important work studying atoms. He was one of the first to realise an atom is made up of a nucleus (in the centre) with charged particles, called electrons, whizzing around it.

MASSIVE BOMB

Super-scientist Albert Einstein is most famous for his equation, $e=mc^2$. It means *energy equals mass times the speed of light squared*. The equation was all about how large amounts of energy could be created from tiny atoms. All you had to do, Einstein said, was to change the atom – easy! Unfortunately, his theory was used to create the atomic bomb which was dropped on the Japanese city of Hiroshima in 1945. Shocked that his scientific discovery had aided such awful mass destruction, Einstein spent the rest of his life campaigning against nuclear weapons.

CAUSING A STINK

Chemists have to deal with some pretty stinky gases. Some of the smelliest are chlorine (in swimming pool water) and methane – the gas that escapes from cows' (and humans') bottoms!

The colour of food seems to affect its taste. Some people prefer egg yolks to be rich yellow and salmon to be deep pink. Farmers often add dyes to make foods look more attractive.

SCIENCE ON A PLATE

Do you eat lactic acid? Oh yes you do – every time you splash milk on to your cornflakes! In fact there's a whole chemistry lab and the results of years of test-tube experiments in your kitchen.

HELLO, DOLLY

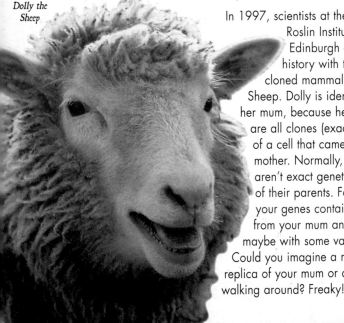

Dolly the Sheep

In 1997, scientists at the Roslin Institute, Edinburgh – made history with the first cloned mammal, Dolly the Sheep. Dolly is identical to her mum, because her genes are all clones (exact copies) of a cell that came from her mother. Normally, offspring aren't exact genetic copies of their parents. For instance, your genes contain a mix from your mum and dad, maybe with some variation. Could you imagine a mini replica of your mum or dad walking around? Freaky!

SQUARE TOMATOES?

Scientists are considering creating square tomatoes that are easy to pack in a box! And how does a straight banana grab you? As farmland gets scarcer, meat may have to be cloned in laboratories instead of having animals grazing in green fields.

Food experiments in the lab

FAT-FREE FOOD

Humans like to eat fat. You may leave fatty bits of meat on your plate, but fats are what make cheese and cakes so delicious. The problem is, if you eat too much fat, *you* become fat! That's why scientists have been searching for something without fat's belt-busting effects. They came up with Olestra. It's at an early stage, but so far it seems to work!

SCIENCE QUIZ

How much food do you eat in a lifetime?

a) no one knows
b) 70 tonnes — the weight of a dozen elephants
c) 35 tonnes — the weight of six elephants

What do calories tell us?

a) how much energy a food contains
b) how much protein a food contains
c) how much fat a food contains

In which film were dinosaurs cloned from DNA?

a) *Jurassic Park*
b) *The Flintstones*
c) *Godzilla*

(answers on page 32)

GENETIC ENGINEERING

You may already have come face to face with evidence of food science – and gobbled it up. Some food plants, such as soya beans, are genetically altered before they are even planted. Scientists might give a plant a gene to make it resistant to weedkiller. This means farmers can spray their fields with toxic chemicals without killing the crop. The problem is, new superweeds may evolve.

ON-SCREEN SCIENCE

As well as test tubes and telescopes, science researchers now use computers to analyse all sorts of data and to make new discoveries about everything from the tiniest atoms to the biggest stars in the universe.

SCIENCE QUIZ

How did Silicon Valley get its name?

a) it has lots of computer software companies
b) it is very sandy
c) silicon is refined there

Where can computer information be stored?

a) on a CD
b) on a zip disk
c) on a hard drive

Who invented the computer?

a) Roger Bannister
b) Albert Einstein
c) Charles Babbage

(answers on page 32)

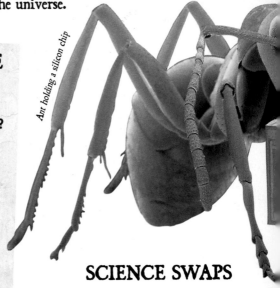

Ant holding a silicon chip

SCIENCE SWAPS

The Internet is very useful for scientists. It has made it easier for them to share new information by publishing research papers on their own web sites. When such papers are published in books and magazines, there isn't space for everyone to have their say. By sharing information, scientists can move forward more quickly than ever before in their search for new questions, answers or products.

THE VIRTUAL STAR

A virtual reality star

In virtual reality (VR), things can be tried safely in a computer-generated environment. Student doctors use VR to practise surgery before they are let loose on real patients! Space scientists use VR to experience the conditions on other planets while staying right here on Earth. VR is used for fun, too – virtual pop star, Kyoko Date, exists only on-screen!

CLEVER CHIPS

The first computers filled whole rooms. Electrical circuits and the means of storing information just had to get smaller. Engineers made them smaller by fitting circuits on to tiny silicon chips. Each circuit might contain millions of components. The size of chips is constantly being reduced. In 1974, engineers could fit nearly 5,000 transistors on a chip. Today, they can fit several million!

SMELLS LIKE TV

Researchers have now developed a smell-releasing microchip that could be built into your TV. You would be able to smell a burger during a commercial, or a flower during a gardening programme!

NUMBER-CRUNCHING

Computers will happily crunch the biggest, most complicated numbers. The fastest can zip through billions of calculations a second. From telescope readings they can produce perfect maps of space. And 3-D modelling on-screen allows scientists to get an all-round view of the newest elements or atomic structures.

QUIZ ANSWERS:

Page 2 a, *Principia*; a, on Earth; c, electrocution.

Page 5 b, 331.3 metres per second; a, Concorde; a, acceleration.

Page 6 b, iron; b, a magnetic field; c, magnetist.

Page 9 a, dynamo; a, amp;-b, amber (they discovered that rubbing two pieces of amber together produced a spark).

Page 10 c, transparent; c, melanin; b, neon and c, fluorescent.

Page 13 a, Ptolemy; a, Sirius (Canis); b, a supernova.

Page 14 b, Search for Extra-Terrestrial Intelligence; c, 1947; c, the distance light travels in a year.

Page 17 c, to block harmful Moon rays – of course! (Moon rays aren't really harmful – Bell just made a mistake). a, Friedrich Mesmer; c, the Sun.

Page 18 a, white blood cells; c, stick-shaped; b, death cap mushroom.

Page 21 c, the *Beagle*; a, southern ape; a, *Miacis*.

Page 22 a, 500 million; a, 288 km/h; b, 1.5 litres.

Page 24 a, the first heart transplant; b, scalpel; b, boiled puppies.

Page 26 a, Jöns Jakob Berzelius; c, Friedrich Kekulé; b, nitrous oxide (sodium chloride is common table salt and lactic acid is milk).

Page 29 c, 35 tonnes; a, how much energy a food contains; a, *Jurassic Park*.

Page 30 a, it has lots of computer software companies; a, b and c, all three are true; c, Charles Babbage.

Acknowledgements

We would like to thank Phil Clucas, Jan Alvey, Helen Wire and Elizabeth Wiggans for their assistance.
Cartoons by John Alston.
Copyright © 2000 *ticktock* Publishing Ltd.
First published in Great Britain by *ticktock* Publishing Ltd.,
The Offices in the Square, Hadlow, Tonbridge, Kent TN11 0DD, Great Britain.

Picture Credits: t = top, b = bottom, c = centre, l = left, r = right, OFC = outside front cover,
OBC = outside back cover, IFC = inside front cover

Holt Studios International; 18/19c. Kobal Collection; 15t. Oxford Scientific Films; 22/23b, 27tr. Photri; 16/17mp.
Pictor International; 2tl, 4/5b, 9tr. Rex; 4cr, 10/11c,17bl, 28bl. Science Photo Library; OFC, IFC, 2/3c, 6t, 8/9c,
10/11mp, 12/13c, 12bl, 14/15mp, 18tl, 20/21, 20/21ct, 22/23c, 24tr, 25r, 26/27t, 28tr, 30/31c.

Picture research by Image Select. Printed in Hong Kong.